habitus

radna fabias

habitus

poems

translated by david colmer

DALLAS, TEXAS

Phoneme Media, an imprint of Deep Vellum
3000 Commerce St., Dallas, Texas 75226
deepvellum.org · @deepvellum

Deep Vellum is a 501c3 nonprofit literary arts organization
founded in 2013 with the mission to bring
the world into conversation through literature.

This publication has been made possible with financial support from the Dutch Foundation for
Literature.

Support for this publication has been provided in part by a grant from the City of Dallas Office of Arts
and Culture's ArtsActivate program, the National Endowment for the Arts, and the Amazon Literary
Partnership.

ISBNs: 978-1-64605-098-7 (paperback) | 978-1-64605-099-4 (ebook)

LIBRARY OF CONGRESS CATALOGING-IN-PUBLICATION DATA

Names: Fabias, Radna, 1983- author. | Colmer, David, 1960- translator.
Title: Habitus : poems / Radna Fabias ; translated by David Colmer.
Other titles: Habitus. English
Description: First edition. | Dallas, Texas : Phoneme Media, Deep Vellum,
  2021.
Identifiers: LCCN 2021021964 (print) | LCCN 2021021965 (ebook) | ISBN
  9781646050987 (trade paperback) | ISBN 9781646050994 (ebook)
Subjects: LCGFT: Poetry.
Classification: LCC PT5882.16.A25 H3313 2021 (print) | LCC PT5882.16.A25
  (ebook) | DDC 839.311/7—dc23
LC record available at https://lccn.loc.gov/2021021964
LC ebook record available at https://lccn.loc.gov/2021021965

Front cover by Justin Childress | justinchildress.co
Interior Layout and Typesetting by KGT

Printed in the United States of America

contents

demonstrable effort made

epilogue

i had a dream in which I saw myself again
in the dark, as I often see myself now
in the dark, moving and searching
the warm hands, the magnifying mirror
that showed my blind self
a ball was my house and it enclosed me
gave me form, but i didn't know that
because i didn't see my form
you are blind with your mother, says the policeman

BERT SCHIERBEEK—*Donkey My Inhabitant*

view with a coconut

what i hid

rims
the impeccably polished rims shining in the sun
                                   too big and too expensive for the cars they spin under

the tinted windows of the cars with the shining rims
the almost horizontal drivers of the cars with the tinted windows and the shining rims
the explosive bass from the subwoofers installed in the trunks
the dust from the dry fields
and pomade: green
or the black version

                                                        smells of oil refinery
                                                                    perfect
                                        for the hair of the modern *neger* in the 1980s
                                                                    perfect
                                    to accentuate the natural blackness, to make it gleam
                                                                    perfect
                                                        for catching the dust

from the dry fields where spiky bushes grow
the dust
carried on the trade wind

                                                        all around and all over

the poky bars
on the side of every road, blacktop or dirt
the women behind the barred windows of the bars on the side of the road
the women
the holes
the women on the streets

                                                        but not after dark

the holes in the road

the men
who drink beer beer beer at the bars on the side of the road sometimes a whisky coke and

finally
find the car
finally
drive off
finally
find the house
finally
get home
finally
find the woman who wasn't drinking at the bar on the side of the road
finally
search for her pussy
and recognize where they are from her pussy
which house it is
which of the many
women
with butts butts butts hoisted into leggings
booties like bumpers on which to hitch to an adjacent island

so they say
women who wear their clothes like a second skin

no such thing as two sizes too small
men with greasy fingers under a makeshift carport next to their house
bent over the engine of a car
sweating beer bottle in hand

that carport's called a garage and
that's a mechanic
when he says shokkashobba
he means shock absorbers
shocks
they wear out so fast there

                                        because of the holes in the road past
men
with clippers and razors under a tree

                                        men like that are called barbers
men who come to collect money

                                        men like that are called arabs
men
under a tree with weapons and whisky

                                        men like that are called thugs
                                                        irresistible

to women
with babes in arms
the smell of their burnt skin
in the sun
the golden sun
the gold teeth
women
whose hair will smell of chemical relaxer for days to come
on top of that the burnt smell of their baked hair

                                        because it has to be smoother
                                        and it doesn't need to be hair

plastic
on the heads and fingers of women
women with curlers
the candy-colored houses
the churches
the churches painted the color of ripe bananas
the tamarind trees
the iguanas
the lizards with half-amputated tails
the free-range goats
the crowing roosters
the dogs chained to trees

the stray dogs that have been run over
the stray dogs asleep under cars that leak oil

the bullets that sound like fireworks

the fireworks to scare off evil spirits
the bullets to scare off evil people
the bullets fired by angry people
the newspapers full of blood
the heavy, throbbing motorcycles ridden by heavies
the old women on the side of the road
selling lottery tickets
selling hope
on the side of the road
by the holes in the road
in the dust
the street kids on undersized bikes
      the way they dance their bikes around girls who have just started menstruating
the mothers who warn about them
the mothers

                                              only
the dust
the lawn in the people who can afford a sprinkler's front yard

                                      greener
the color of the people who can afford a sprinkler

                                 lighter than
the junkie in the people who can afford a sprinkler's front yard
the stuff under the junkie's arm in the people who can afford a sprinkler's front yard
the deep black color of the street junkie with the thickly callused feet

                                  natural sandals
the wrecked cars
the litter
the thirsty earth

the apocalyptic downpours
the wind
the hurricanes
the telenovelas
                              the silicone breasts of the women in the telenovelas
the bloody news from nearby countries
the beauty pageants
                              the silicone breasts of miss venezuela

the native language
the official language
the unofficial language
the unofficially segregated supermarkets
the unofficially segregated schools
the decapitated rooster in the woman across the road's backyard
the woman across the road's tarot cards
the woman across the road's incense
the incense in the banana-yellow churches
the churches
the fortune-tellers
the brujas who serve the gamblers
the gambling
                              tomorrow maybe win tomorrow maybe win
the sweating bodies rubbing up against each other
                              that's called dancing

the heat
the washcloth in the bus driver's pocket
the fans blowing hot air
the processions of mournful people
the people who throw themselves on a loved one's coffin and scream
                              that's called mourning
the cemeteries where human remains are shelved one on top of the other
the women's voices saying the rosary
the transistor radio

the women's voices on the transistor radio saying the rosary
hail marys
our fathers
the raised voices of the people on the transistor radio
the dj talking through the songs on the transistor radio
the requests the dj talks right through on the transistor radio
the sudden falling of the night
the justified fear in the night
the ghosts
the rippling blacktop
the lack of escape routes
the lack of seasons
the lack

the way everything is surrounded by sea
the way everything is scorched by the sun

the horror
the tourists

                                        always smile at tourists
                                        that's called manners

the sun
the blue
the impossible blue of the sky
the impossible blue of the sea
the fishermen in boats floating on the impossibly blue, transparent sea
the sand
the washed-up fish tails on the white sand
the white sand against the impossible blue of the sea
the white sand that looks suspiciously like the dust
the dust

opening scene

at the airport i take off
my shoes my belt and if
they ask my pants as well

i submit to being sniffed by dogs the weapons
are in my fingertips where i
have also stored my rapid heartbeat

i look smart i've done my hair
i smile like a sheep keep my eyes

on the floor the elastic
of the mask behind my ears

travel guide I

you can dive there if you are not afraid of depth
swim with dolphins if you suppress cruelty
to animals with a scene from a movie
where freedom rides on a whale's back

int. motherland – night

transplanted palms now cast nimble shadows on the bed i'm lying on
don't ask me if i'm scared

the shadow of the cactus that is native there is a stationary phallus on the wall
opposite the bed i'm lying on
don't ask me if i'm scared

the wind blows through the holes in the roof above the bed i'm lying on
i don't believe in ghosts
don't ask me anything

the sea is deep
i stash the fear in the pebbles

travel guide II

you can
in the heart of want
see an ingenious bridge slide over the water in the harbor and act
like functional man-made constructions can
be a cathartic experience you do
need to fake it a little

is, is like

the returned migrant is like
the returned migrant is is
the hot air the succumbing to the heat
is the succumbing

the returned migrant is the adult is
the motherland that is the mother he tries
to worm back into is the worming is hot is blood everywhere
is the midwife the sigh
"it's painful for everyone"

the returned migrant is the bar-slash-grocery store is
the booze in the hand of the drunk is
the drunk in the same corner on the same chair is the same
diabetic drunk who sat there years ago too the returned migrant is
paralyzed on that same chair is that chair is phantom pain observes
the amputation

the returned migrant is the ocean is a few steps away from the ocean a small hot church
the hot air a handful of plastic fans that blow the hot air to and fro the returned migrant
looks for answers sits with a missal on his knee is the missal is here together in the name
of the Father the Son et cetera sings together with the burnt bodies is the voices is the
bodies is the Father the Son et cetera is the songs he learned before he knew how to
ask interlocking questions the returned migrant is interlocking questions and the heat
is a few steps away from the ocean is just like that water just like that water the returned
migrant is full of terror inducing life is frightening is frightened is
deep
blue
dark

the returned migrant hears himself the wind the water hears the wind and the water's
whispered death threats is all this is his neighbor is a small hot church is the hot air
is the host is the kneeler is a few steps away from the ocean is the ocean is next to the
church is the donkey is a vacant lot where the donkey brays chained to a lamppost
during holy communion is the donkey is the vacant lot
is the eyes is
torn the returned migrant is
his eyes closes
his eyes closes
himself is closed
prays
is the prayer to be whole

travel guide III

you can visit the churches, which are actually the same as the churches you already know
but brightly colored
to distract from
the shame and the blood
on the walls

you can, as you're already there anyway,
view the sand in a relatively old synagogue as if
the whole island isn't surrounded by it
maybe even made of it
act as if
judaism too is something you care about

the laying on of hands

it's hot again
sister rita has done her best, but it won't cool off
(the a/c blows warm air on the overheated women)
the church is heaven's waiting room
that bodes well

the lady in front of me is wearing a feather hat
(under the hat a wig)
the Holy Spirit just knocked her down
(the hat slid off her head)
i keep my eyes on the wig
(she's lying in front of the dais, speaking in tongues)

this is the church brother george built

the fallen lady shivers as if winter exists here
she jerks
(porn for God-fearing women)

all the widows spinsters discontinued brides in heat now lying
next to each other as the new front row
(their wigs their hats)
two pairs of dented ovaries drape blankets over the ladies' lower bodies and their tears
(they jerk pant writhe some cry out)

brother george has run his hand over the glowing body parts of at least three women
(yet we only honor the church he built)

in heaven's waiting room we keep our legs pressed tightly together
(me too, Father, me too)
nobody is obsessed with the flesh of all the men who have ever preached here
(and definitely not me, Lord, not me)

brother george pulls it out and it is holy because Christ
too was made flesh and He bore it with dignity

travel guide IV

for a few guilders you can also
buy the fiction of the carefree caribbean
from a black man who has mastered a discreet kind of cynicism so discreet
you won't recognize it at first and maybe
he doesn't either

for the experience he drives an open vehicle with fat tires suited to rougher
terrain on a faraway continent and despite the absence
of wild animals he still calls it a "safari"

for a modest surcharge, he will drive you
to bay one, bay two, bay three
he'll pull over for a photo break at bay four
where you will find a modest line of red people
taking photos of each other
with the blue in the background
for the pale folk at home shivering
under the yoke of winter

at the last stop—the salt pans—he smiles
at how the flamingos stand there sleeping
while the travelers wrestle with electronic devices
that is his favorite metaphor

three ways i am or know the sea

I
i am brown and water
splashes against my edges
i leave a trail on the path
—i've been walking it for years—
behind me someone keeps complaining how slippery it is—mostly a man—
i say "that's the tears"
i know it's the sea

(sometimes i say
"it's the rain"
that too is a lie
it is always the sea)

II
i am blue
i am an absolutely angry blue
on the surface i ripple gently
i give misshapen monsters
a home i am not sorry
my tongue is salty

III
i love a good rock
black and hard and full of secrets
i am made of water
i am water
i let myself be whipped up by the wind
i love a good rock
i polish its edges

travel guide v

the juiciest lie is splendor there is
the yacht club there are
cuban cigars there is
mediocre yet pricey imported whisky and
there is cognac

the golf resorts maintained with excessive quantities of desalinated seawater
green scars
in the natural landscape

red people and those who want to belong with them
are driven around in golf carts by
beaming *negers*
according to the terms of their employment

for the very wealthiest there is also the lie
that this is enough
this lie requires constant repurchasing
it runs out fast it never satisfies
but converted to your own currency it's still dirt cheap

view with a coconut (in soviet montage)

the sun rises over the flowering tropical landscape but elsewhere
in a dark parking lot somebody brings a baseball bat down on the windshield of a car

the tropics turn orange yellow orange yellower but
somebody keeps calling and crying

the dawn is noble and the dawn is honest but
somebody has to pay for a crushed skull and agrees to a payment plan

a black woman (old) in the middle of the road (hot) says "you could fry an egg on this" but
somebody sniffs and plunges their face in the snow

somebody runs out onto the street with a charred heart and clenched fists looking for war
somebody cuts a pile of shirts into little triangles as if hypnotized
somebody kicks somebody else's pet
somebody pushes somebody else onto tracks at night where a train arrives an hour later
somebody breaks
somebody breaks a cell phone in two
somebody drags a key over somebody else's window and makes a black promise

somebody steals something
somebody steals somebody

the blossom is soft and the blossom consoles
but somebody fiddles a bent coat hanger into a keyhole in a dark doorway
somebody swears
somebody keeps calling and breaking
somebody rips open on the floor of an apartment on the eighteenth floor next to the
tracks that carry

night trains that make the floor shake
somebody drinks red wine from a box
somebody gets flames tattooed over somebody else's name
somebody drops a pipe
somebody falls

the sea is blue and the sea embraces me
but somebody is having convulsions
somebody is hallucinating a busty goddess in camouflage clothing
somebody is hearing voices
somebody is drinking champagne and tears
somebody is in mourning with a dutch donut and a ramses shaffy chanson
somebody sniffs and throws himself on the powdered sugar
somebody falls into a deep sleep in the water

the sky is bright and the land is green and i push
against the front door with all my weight but they're already inside
the wrecks the lifeless
objects that once were people
i know it stinks because i'm holding my hand over my nose

the light shines on the flowering tropical landscape but
the hero bursts in the very place he thought he would be whole

the tropics flower in the golden landscape
but we see close-ups of torn scars
the shots are subtitled:
"blood"
"grazes"
"swelling"
"contusions"

the sun shines on the hero
the hero has burst open
something crawls out of him
we can't see what it is
there is the sun
the camera zooms out
the sun is still there
the correspondent on the battlefield
the sun is there too
the correspondent turns to stone
the sun reveals its stubborn streak
above the flowering tropical landscape
the correspondent shrugs

somebody has been waiting at the window for a very long time

father

and the old man went to the sea and the old man didn't catch anything and the old man found his insignificance

capital

we find the inheritance in moldy boxes that have been yellowing for at least four
generations in the house under our great-grandmother's skin, under the skin of all her
progeny

i get
five tricks to make slot machines pay out
a simple way to make money
eight ways to stop your man from straying including
four potions for a tighter cunt
a recipe for stay-put water
and a book that has been faithfully updated over the years with lifesaving instructions
for the defenseless wench in which i read:

fan incense over your man when he's asleep
if it's just the tip, you'll never get pregnant and
the first inch won't depreciate you anyway
MAKE SURE to turn off your phone before three in the morning because of radiation from
mars that causes alzheimer's
don't buy bread at the supermarket (it's made with human hair and white people have
been baking mice into the heart of our bread for years)
BE CAREFUL generic drugs are part of a complex conspiracy that is almost impossible to
explain but definitely put your life at risk don't take them live long WATCH OUT
if you put your handbag on the floor you'll stay poor forever
if someone sweeps your feet you will never marry, and by the way, you didn't hear this
from me, but if you forward this message to at least fifteen friends, you'll get a year's
worth of transatlantic phone credit IT'S TRUE live long phone long BE CAREFUL yoga is a
tool of the devil, but stay supple: that too will keep your man from straying
if you share this message with at least twenty people, you'll get an end-of-year bonus of
$10,000 from a giant software corporation IT'S TRUE a friend of a friend got it he went
on vacation with the money

BE CAREFUL if you put your feet up on the table, your mother will die

that sound at the front door is Jesus knocking to come and live in your heart GOD BLESS

give money to the church every week OR ELSE

this is a photo of a wicked man who uses a story about starving children in west africa

to try to get into your house to rob it WATCH OUT don't let him in and more generally

speaking if you don't want someone to ever come back into your house, throw a handful

of salt after them when they leave TAKE CARE

burn sage

on new year's eve jump back and forth three times over hot coals you've sprinkled with

incense then sacrifice fireworks to the evil spirits so they'll leave you alone for the rest of

the year

on the dot of midnight eat twelve grapes, one for each month of the year

(it's not clear what this gets you, but better do it anyway)

if you do not share these instructions there's a real chance of your children dying within

four months

if you don't have children your lover

if you don't have a lover your parents

if you no longer have parents your self

in passing

the mass of a car racing over the asphalt
collides with the body of a dog
the uninsured driver keeps driving
with a dog-shaped dent in his car

the dog is still yelping

the dying dog is now run over repeatedly by a succession of vehicles
the sound of breaking bones rises up in the clear blue sky over the asphalt
over the motionless dog

the dog sighs out its life

the dead dog is now lying in the heat
it's like the dog has fallen asleep in its own blood

now the dog starts to swell

the dog now seems to be overweight
two of the four crushed legs pointing up at the sky

the dog is swollen

now the swollen dog explodes
the dead dog's warm intestines leap out of its body
leaving the dead dog a husk

the dog's crushed carcass now looks like a drained blood balloon or a very filthy rug

the stench rises up in the clear blue sky over the asphalt
over the motionless dog

the dog is now surrounded by flies

postcard

dear,

i have put my ear to the sea (as instructed), but i only heard the shifting of the sand

treasure

the fortune-teller asks me what has brought me here i say
the winter homesickness fictional hopelessness and an inability to amputate my cultural
background from my identity
she predicts that i will find my treasure in a person i ask
is it a man or a woman or someone else or is it the unruly child i don't want to bear it will be
a boy with curls of fire i saw it in a dream he's going to get girls who are sweet but not
too clever pregnant and abandon them he can't help it it's in his blood

a person, she says, the treasure is in a person
i ask if it's me she says certainty is in the church
but i've already been baptized on land at sea and in the air with fire and fire and ash and water
my doubt is stubborn
all i have is hope and sometimes
love
the rest has been burned down

i offer her my hand and a cup of cigarette ash to the value of three hundred euros
i give her my wrists i beg
fathom my chakras feel my energy or my heartbeat study the whites
of my eyes palpate my pressure points stir my qi feed my hope but again she says
your treasure is in a person

she says i have to go home

she says she doesn't speak my language

closing scene

at the airport i pluck
my forearms i shave
until I'm smooth i scrub
myself clean only under
my nails the earth i dug
i swallowed what i found

i am half a ton heavier
i love my girth
i am more naked than allowed
i pick up my panties

the scan analyst nods me on
my cavities are empty
the final inspection shows that i'm not wearing anything explosive under my skirt
i am not dangerous

the hollow doesn't get inspected
there is a rustling in my cavities
my cavities are empty

nobody noticed, but i stepped out of my skin and i was naked and i was sinew muscle vein

i was red

rib

Enormous room. Ophelia. Ihr Herz ist eine Uhr.

HEINER MÜLLER—*Die Hamletmachine*

inspection on arrival

roughly 5'7" if the measuring instrument compacts the hair
springy hair (fine, curly, stiff in places, changeable, thirsty)
forehead: not prominent
eyebrows: black—partly joined—
eyelashes: not counted, she's got them, they're dark
eyes: large, dark brown, conspicuously present as is
nose: conspicuously ethnic
lips: almost no pout, corners of mouth rise fairly regularly
teeth: slightly damaged by biting hard objects, wisdom teeth removed by force
tongue: damaged, blames love
chin: depending on angle of appraisal, single
throat: intact
shoulders: hard
back: burdened
collarbones: not prominent
breasts: marked by savage human hands—no visible damage—
birthmarks: god's spit
belly: round with promise, not with child
buttocks: fairly curved—less bulk than the bloodline might predict—
haunted pelvis
hips: broad
legs: muscular from military operations
feet: flat, always touch the ground
arms: heavy
heavy-handed

incarnation

in the beginning was the hole and the hole had already been dug
unless observation leads to guilt, i was not an accomplice

she—the lioness—sighed and i was there
(inhumanly tender, searchlight eyes)
she wrapped me in a golden blanket that had been fashioned to look noble but was
actually made from the leather of a dairy cow that had been milked dry then brutally
slaughtered for my wellbeing and warmth
her breath caught she called it love it seemed a lot like fear
the gold blanket cracked and everyone could see the skin of the slaughtered cow
highly embarrassing

tears were shed
it was not clear if those present were crying because of the cow or
the violence involved or
about my fingers, which were apparently made to play pianos
nobody there could afford
we were sure that one of them was crying about the symmetry of my eyebrows
the source of the rest of the sorrow was less transparent
let's just say there was a lot and it was briny

she—the lioness—was lying on a bed
the bed had become an island in a sea of unidentifiable tears
someone was swimming away from me
the midwife protested
nobody was paying attention to my umbilical cord but somebody said

this is mainland
always stay on the mainland always keep
your eyes on the horizon always look
for signal fires

                                        i had other people's tears in my ears
                            i couldn't hear properly, so i always looked for fire
                                                when i wanted to go home

i let myself be molded
that's how the first misunderstanding arose after three or four moldings nobody knew
what my original shape had been
i could never become myself again and no one recognized me anywhere

when they found me—years later—the headlines said

BESMIRCHED EXOTIC BEAUTY
(WELL YEAH WHAT IS BEAUTY)
FOUND AT THE HEART-BLACK BOTTOM OF THE WELL

                                        the journalists forgot i had a mother
                                and my mother too and her mother before her
                                        they wanted to know what happened
                    i was invited onto a quiz show to choose the best answer to that question
                                        i chose "persistent patrimony"

that won a balding provincial fortysomething a suitcase containing 50,000 banknotes
currency from a country that no longer exists
                                        the host asked me to turn around

the balding provincial gent used both hands to shoot the useless banknotes at my ass
meanwhile the host sang a song about the beauty of holland in the rain

                                        the laugh track was on

a blond woman yelled that it was just what i deserved
her fury, metropolitan and delphic

the cameraman was just in time to capture a tear
he too forgot my mother and her mother and her mother and the absent fathers
while pressing the microphone up against my lips

the bald man kept shooting banknotes at my ass

the laugh track was still on

it made for two minutes of excellent television

adam washes ashore

sunday morning on the church square
in the city—autumn leaves on the ground
the authorities have abolished
coincidence—i pick him up i pat him
dry i keep him for his own sake around
him i write a sentence his backpack fits into

adam stretches drowning
has done him good how clean
he is he has six masks he is
wearing one he's saved
from the desert where he was
alone still intact and dry

(great-)grandmotherly advice

dead bodies are heavy
you're better off not trying
to transport them on bicycles over the damp slippery christmas-lit cobbles of a medium-sized
western city where people are walking through shops in search of things to buy death
is the last thing those people are looking for
they've already got it
it's not new

you're also better off not keeping dead bodies in your belly
especially not between your vital organs
unless you want to speed decay of course
but child you never need to lend decay a helping hand

never trust
a fisherman
never trust
an islander
never trust
an official
never trust
a libra—they can't make up their minds—

never get involved with *negers* who wear their dreads up on their heads in knotted pantyhose
—that is a metaphor—
never get involved with *negers* who compulsively unthinkingly grab their dicks
—that too is a metaphor—
never trust anyone the color of bittersweet chocolate
—you'll never get them off your thighs—

never trust a man don't
trust anyone trust me

quiet considerations (in the dark)

the beauty of snakeskin is only perceptible to those who have no fear
of phallic shapes or snakelike movements

fear muffles beauty
that in turn casts light on the rarity of beauty

defilers are better than average at consent they don't need anyone
else to get involved that explains the violence
of violation it also explains why the excellent consenter does not experience
any resistance worth mentioning, besides the thrashing
perhaps, but
thrashing is yes
tensing is yes
every audible reaction is yes
the petrified body says yes
aversion is a mild form of revulsion and therefore yes
revulsion is also yes
sleep is yes
disbelief is yes
dry is yes
wet is yes
so a cold sweat is yes
dissociation is yes anger
is yes tears
are yes yes was always a superfluous luxury
and silence is consent

if seen from the right angle being dishonored is a form of winning, right?
this does raise questions about the word dishonor because isn't it an honor
to not be left untouched?

no
is yes if i say
that i will never understand the beauty of snakeskin i mean it's fine
for a python to strangle me swallow me
because three times no is yes yes definitely yes
you bet

or
a quiet room
where things break

the blackness of the hole

black holes are weird
black holes are the strangest
objects in the universe

a planet or star has a surface a black hole is black so black a black hole doesn't have a surface
a black hole is an area a hole in space an area where matter is
compressed and
catastrophically collapsed

cat-a-clys-mic

that fatal collapse concentrates an enormous quantity of mass in a very very very small area
the gravity in this area is
black
very black and strong
so strong nothing can escape it
light almost always escapes but not from a black hole objects
that fall into black holes break everything
that falls into the black hole breaks everything
that falls into the black hole is stretched to the breaking point

once an astronaut came too close to a black hole he was sucked into it he was torn apart
by the superhuman enormity of the gravity in the hole let that be a lesson to us nasa said
we can't see black holes but we believe in their existence just like we believe in Jesus
nasa said we believe the black hole because the black hole does things to matter
because the black hole does things to stars because the black hole does things to the
solar systems in the vicinity of the black hole the black hole doesn't think about it the
black hole acts according to its nature

the hole is an area in space
the hole is black
the hole is catastrophically collapsed matter
black
a gravity grave
the hole is often surrounded by disks of matter
the disks rotate in a vortex around the black hole and get god-awful hot

rib

embrace your fate, rib

trail your fingers over your legs feel your fur remove your fur strip what is too much and
turn on the falsetto

draw a black line under your eyes calm down act calm draw the outline of the woman
you must become on your hips

shrink

let someone else's breath scrape softly over the spot that's bruised softly damaging your
throat softly

show the pain and if it doesn't hurt, not really, look like it hurts look like death
is on your heels

sigh

and groan

but not too loud

confirm the presumed defenselessness

don't make too much eye contact

lower your eyes in slow motion

look up

only use the corners of your mouth

purse your lips

not more than two seconds but purse them

briefly

shrink

smaller

whoa

not too small

you have to stay visible make yourself lighter a little bit more

lighter still cultivate patience restrain yourself

have some manners

let yourself be undressed be

liftable be

malleable show yourself
penetrable and eager
a little eagerness is allowed
be eager now
stop

hoist yourself slowly into the cuirass
the cuirass is made of death and honey you're dripping
deadcoldhoneysweet
feel the shame
now learn to wait

bride

like many women i always knew i would marry a man a black man
as that would go better with my dress
a question of contrast

the ceremony took place in a church dedicated to a faith i do not adhere to
the priest like all the female guests wore a veil
white
he ended his sermon by asking who was going to call the police

on the altar were objects i knew from my childhood
a cactus, glowing coals, an axe for doing the weeding and a dead animal
presumably a stray dog

the floor was covered with corn flour
the interior recalled a beach bar
the incense smelled like midnight mass

the priest drew a seawater cross on my ash-covered forehead
i promised eternity in a language i didn't speak
i had only learned that one sentence

the bridegroom said the language didn't matter
everyone there looked vacant in a very specific way

i wasn't wearing a bra and was embarrassed by the nipple imprints in my lie
in my white white lie of a wedding dress
my groom whispered that marriage is a formality
for the reassurance of those who gave us birth

the women sang a song about my lost innocence
i apologized
it was a long sit
my veiled mother-in-law thanked me in advance for the grandchildren

on the way out the guests pelted us
with a range of seeds and grains: aniseed for a sweet wedding night—as if we needed
it—then rice—because that was the done thing—then black dead-black sesame seed
according to my groom an important symbol and just before we left the church on the
doorstep, buckwheat

old story with magical and imaginary beings and events

the first room we don't sleep in is a hollow tree
we are termites
we eat our way in, touching the darkness
your termite voice tells me the moors brought civilization to the west i ask where do you
stand
on the discussion regarding the ethnicity of the Messiah our Lord Jesus Christ you say
He was black of course but the rest of that story is incorrect

you're not looking properly
i am incorrect
i'm not blaming you
termites are blind

the second room we don't sleep in is a space shuttle we are aliens
i take your feelers for tentacles and vice versa
we are repulsive
we are cosmic
we are moist
you tell me you once knew an astronaut who was destroyed in a black hole
you're forgetting the event horizon you take chaos for demolition i   don't say it

the next room is a volcano but i can take it
the heat eats away half of your face and then i see you
sharp
angular
frightened

in the fourth there's a bed at long last but the desk and bedside cabinets are suspended
upside down from the ceiling the new testament
could come crashing down on us at any moment
you offer me the other cheek and i lick it

in the fifth room you cup your hands come here stay here we'll have to get married you explain us you tell me i'm fluid and you love it when things flow through you i say of course i am black but the rest of that story is incorrect

the sixth room we don't sleep in is between the lobby and the breakfast room the receptionist looks at the telephone but doesn't pick up in the breakfast room hard-boiled eggs have been arranged on a metal tray on a bed of coffee beans
don't ask us why
someone outside has moved the city
which is now floating on the clouds
it looks ridiculous

for the last room we have to walk quite a distance from the parking lot to reach reception the tiles in the bathroom are falling off the shower leaks there is hair in the drain the window won't open the a/c is too noisy the quilts are too short when breakfast in bed arrives it's almost lunchtime the bacon is chewy the scrambled eggs soupy the coffee watery the pipes are moldy something's dripping out of the wallpaper there's no kettle there aren't any bathrobes the hair dryer doesn't work the sauna is only open for one hour every other day you have to call them first so they can turn it on it takes at least half an hour to warm up and doesn't smell of eucalyptus at all

and the bed
is too soft

the desolation of borderlands

we take the highway through the desert driving past hundreds maybe thousands of
cactuses it's a long way my goodness
what a long way and halfway I start wondering
if we'll ever get there if it's safe if we're not racing toward our deaths in our vehicle
an el camino
red and gleaming
in the dry country
under bright blue sky

we're burning

i lay my hand on your crotch you keep your eyes on the road you press your foot down
we're nowhere we're surrounded by cactuses the wind blows your smile over to the pas-
senger seat into my lap i joke about wile e coyote and the road runner tell you about the
dubbed spanish version where he's called correcaminos it is indescribably hot you too
are hot you are perfect you are something to flee to you are one of God's wonders you
flash your big white teeth the wind keeps tossing your curling lips into my lap and in
the rearview mirror my head is rolling over the road bigger and bigger but also farther
and farther away

tumbleweed

i don't need to eat drink sleep i want it
on the rippling blacktop the hot hot blacktop right
on the yellow stripe where i'm at
home in the middle of the road
under the bright blue sky
in the cruel sun let's do it
on the hood let's

do it with the steering wheel jammed in my back and your hands in my hair gently
lean me forward push my head into the trunk laugh sweetly while you're at it say
keep that head cool
and touch me
from behind

i write letters to concerned friends and relatives
"the sun shines here too
the land is not surrounded by sea
the wind is no respite
you would have liked it here
i think of cactuses
i think of cactus
i think of cacti
i was a cloverleaf of deserts
a natural maze
now i'm gone
now i'm fire
now i'm here
to find me
follow the smell of burning the smoke and ash"

war

i go out stealing with my enemy
but only from large organizations
he says the r at the start of your name isn't for robin hood but r kelly
but we're all adults here and i only steal from large organizations

my enemy doesn't believe in my innocence
but together we steal swedish flatbread from a furniture store
so he probably has a point

i share a bottle with my enemy on the dance floor i stumble
through the night i look
death but especially madness in the eye i wink at them
death madness my enemy he has the most beautiful eyes
brown, like ditchwater
in those eyes i am not a beautiful person
but everyone looks dirty in ditchwater and
on a scale from 1 to 10
he gives my ass a 48

i sit with my enemy at sidewalk cafés he breathes
his fictional certainty in and out my enemy is alive
he doesn't need oxygen when no one's looking
he slides a straw into my backbone and slowly, slowly slurps me up
because my enemy thinks i'm delicious

i cook meals rich in carbohydrates with my enemy
he piles starch on starch because he knows so much about war
i dance again with my enemy until it grows light
dehydrated i lie down to recover reminded of how
to suffer with a hand in someone else's pants and
i smoke i burn i breathe fire again we set
floors beds sofas stools chairs aflame

flames licking wardrobes doors walls under the watchful eyes
of neighbors on the backs of innocent women
and dangling over the chasm of course
that's a given when you do it with the enemy

it's good to sleep next to the enemy a mother once said
but it's much better to sleep with the enemy
though it's not a pretty sight because in this gloom
he doesn't have a face and his shadow
looks like mine

action

the lights go out so this must be a movie
the opening scene will later turn out to be deceptive
but that is dramatic irony the main character doesn't know yet

in the first scene, between dead objects on a dead set: a person
a man with receding temples and a mullet
on the floor

the voice-over tells us that addicts tend to maintain the look of the era in which they
became addicted the picture is murky and supports this claim by also getting stuck

this is definitely a movie because there are shards and there is a bang

we see the man dragging his bones through the room
we see the man breaking his own bones
we see a high-strung cat that is afraid of fire
a hysterically shrieking parakeet
a hand hurling crockery and a cellophane-wrapped fruit basket full of candy and custard
tard
for the addict
for his sorrow

without it being clear why, a directorial voice-over intrudes on the dialogue
postmodernism is in play everyone talking at cross-purposes or to the wall
there is no catharsis because there is no hero

the director now says that clichés do not exist so it must be a documentary he says
the shards are real and so is the tarnished tinfoil
nothing rhymes so it must be real

the enraged addict demolishes the windows the winter cold enters the room his heart now shows a hairline fracture we hear the jangling of the warder's keys philosophically speaking the man is still a prisoner he has never been free we realize that now

we see a frightened young woman with rough edges her insides
cotton candy eiderdown the coat of a purring cat
but we don't find out until the final scene

04:40

there was no wall the wall that wasn't there didn't fall
the man with the sketchy moustache is not a dictator and that is not a moustache
there were no explosives it wasn't a war nothing blew up

exorcism

i hit him repeatedly—rhythmically—on the shoulders with a bunch of twigs when he's back
i make sure the room i do this in smells of bruised roses and cunt juice
he will say he's lost something something has left him he will suspect me
how dare he
i forgive him

i hum a lullaby and praise him: he is reborn
i search around him
where he once had a body i stroke what has been
lost with my fingertips
this is my man, sister:
rising again from custody stumbling again doing more time and rising once more
i make the sign of the cross for him and call him Jesus

i carefully wash the buzz of unfreedom out of his ears so the sound of my keys no longer
terrifies him

i praise him
i make sure he's lying down while i do this
i make sure to kneel while doing this

i scrub his wrists i whisper
to his lungs about oxygen
i move all the furniture for his comfort the curtains must never be drawn again he needs a
clear view of every window and i have to become transparent so he can see right through
me too

i tell him that claustrophobia is a lie
i hold him back when he wants to go out at night
i hold tight to his feet
i drive out

the suicidal tendencies with my breasts my cracks i am
his hollow

i sprinkle his body with brown sugar and pray he'll be sweet
over the bed over him over his thoughts i scatter wilted flowers i gathered in the fields
—confetti for my patient and his terror—

i clean the guilt from his belly
i do this thoroughly
i scour him raw
the skin will grow back

i say "easy now" when i mean "i don't know why i'm still here"
i never again compare myself to the wind
i hurl myself on him like a waterfall

i tell him the sorrow had settled in my belly
i had to wash wash wash
i show him
how little it helped

i show him my new cheekbones collarbones hipbones
never had i seen myself like this before
i say "through you for you i have shrunk"
my voice is free of reproach

i hide his guilt behind my eyes where nobody comes
i hide the questions there too
you know
"what now"
if love is reduction
how small can a woman become

i get his twelve street names tattooed in two straight lines
from my breasts to my ankles
i say "now i am locked"

i wash him until he's asleep
when i run out of water i use spit

i ignore the stench
this is my man, sister, this is no grave

when he's asleep
when he's finally asleep
i nestle into his torso so he no longer misses his rib

statement

ex as in ex-con as in that which has no poetry inside of it
inside
as in doing time the way one does time in the pen
pen
as in write the way you write someone off
off
as in kill the way a predator kills its prey
prey
as in vulnerable
as in something that can bleed as in not him
him
as in not her
her
as in hurt
as in taken
as in history repeating itself
as in cliché
as in she had to call every *neger* in town to make sure his supply was topped up
typical
as in they were all wearing the same quilted coats with fur collars in hot weather
coats
for the conveyance of narcotics and other secrets
secrets
as in what makes brothers strut or what's called godlessness in other places
called
as in given a name
a name
as in a vehicle for shame
shame
as in longing for dark

dark
as in a place to hide
hide
as in where he is, she isn't
being there
as in defeating fear
present
as in not having fled
as in
a weapon
loaded
cold
sleeping quietly
hidden from view
by a pair of lace panties

guidelines for revenge

call it by its name: beast
wear your crown

learn everything about force-feeding
wear your crown

make a voodoo doll
three-legged
watch it strut
wear your crown

for at least ten years let the fury
encrust nails grow
take a lot of calcium
leave the tower

file your nails at night when you wake up—calmly—until your hands are rakes
wear your crown

slice the dragon open with your rakes
(pointed sexy sharp and fierce)
wear your glittering party dress

say
"but you have words, beast, use them"
wear your crown

make it squat make it
cough until it gives back
what wasn't his

what we are able to report about the circumstances

first corinthians 13 of course

the circumstances are asymmetric

the romantic variant of the circumstances is often ushered in by a strange
desire that generally does not last as long as the circumstances

regardless of moral position it is always classier to spare the challenger the following:
corners and other parts of the packaging of contraceptives not used in his or her presence
pity
doubt

certainty is inadvisable given the circumstances

there are men who storm silently
they are named after wild
animals kings prophets dictators gods
it is advisable
to board up the windows sandbag the door unplug electronic devices
try not to leave them around ovulation

there are women who are terrifyingly warm all
contact with their lower body causes implosion

sensitivity follows injury in contact
with heat sources blisters sting

the circumstances are fluid

the circumstances are spillable

the circumstances are subject to gravity

gieser wildeman

gieser wildeman is a stewing pear
i am a woman
that is the roof of a three-hundred-year-old house
i am a woman
that is the cloudy liquid running down his chin from a spanish peach and unfortunately i
am
the liquid and the peach and every other soft sweet juicy piece of fruit because i am
a woman and those are the frames of the glasses of a man of average intelligence, but i am
a woman and sufficient in myself
there is no emptiness inside me
there is a hiding place a front room a waiting room a place
where i can receive someone
a man
the start of a child
a woman's fingers
still i am sufficient to myself it doesn't matter
how much postmodern gender theory i hump
around it still shows: i am a woman i could exist beside a man but a man is not a body
a man is not rumbling bass tones not a low voice big arms stiff fingers thick skin not a
beard a man is not a beard a man is not purgatory a man is not a destiny a man is not a
house to live in a man is not a bed to lie on a man is not job creation not a distraction not
occupational therapy a man is not a thoroughbred a man is more than worshipful eyes in
a stolen night a man is not the trunk of a car not a siren a man is not a deep bow before
my crotch a man
has feelings too
he has thoughts
can be hurt
sometimes he even knows why he's hurting
a man
is not
 a meat hook not a filleting knife not a gun not a branding iron not a holy book
a man is not a weapon not a hobby

a man is not a hobby
a man is not a hobby
a man is not a hobby

a man is not a punishment not a line i have to write a hundred times
a man is not a throne to sit on legs crossed like a lady
i am not a lady
i am a woman

demonstrable effort made

It's all good, baby baby.

THE NOTORIOUS B.I.G.—*Juicy*

when the cold comes

you have to grab the snow feel the cold
in your fingertips in your tense shoulders in your limbs
to understand winter you have to taste the snow the snow
must be metabolized into tears the process
is incomprehensible unscientific irreproducible
there is no other way

scum

first i lifted up a high-rise
home to 436 turks
shoes at the front doors
i tried to keep the building vertical so that the residents wouldn't
be inconvenienced by the tilting gravity
i was brought up considerate

then i lifted up the cruising zone and rolled it out around turktown
unfortunately a few trans ladies slipped down past the windows
calling out to me in spanish
heartrending

with my bare hands i unscrewed the metal benches in the public spaces tossing them
on the pile on my back with the stolen bicycles the homeless people who came with
them the roofless the people who confused drifting with traveling the suicidal the train
tracks the lampposts and all the graffiti-smeared overpasses

i picked up the snipes the roaches the grains of coke on the toilet roll holders in the
public bathrooms the lighters the delighters the fire-setters the bums the bridge they
sleep under their improvised crack pipes a handful of needles the lonely freaks in porn
theaters and all the worn-out shoes

everything stuck together with body fluids

my back creaked
the people trembled
because i was brought up considerate i made a coat from the ties of all the unhappy
businessmen i had scraped off the street on friday night
i wrapped the coat around
the civilian casualties
the taxi drivers
the night porters

the cleaners
the sleepless welfare recipients i shed
a single tear from each of their eyes and i carried the street that was mine because it fitted
on my back

you hear stories

"they're coming to grope the women seduce the men harvest gold their nails are black from the pits they dig for others they guzzle"

"they guzzle gin to warm their reptile bodies catch hail in cups to cool their drinks they are superhuman"

"they are superhuman their umbilical cords were never cut, long thick tough 8,000 miles long stretched tight across the ocean"

"their umbilical cords are 8,000 miles long stretched tight across the ocean their children are tightrope walkers only the bravest dare follow the path back home many discover too late that the rope is slack"

"few make it home"

nothing to it

working magic with cocaine and ammonia
letting the brew cool off
separating the brew
divvying up the solid and weighing it on olive-drab digital scales:
craft

cutting the corners off sandwich bags
putting the weighed quantities in the sandwich-bag corners
twisting the open end to make a little ball in the sandwich-bag corner
scorching the twist with a lighter that produces a remarkably large flame
repeat
rapping along to fiddy
repeat:
mass production

slipping the bags into a coat
putting on the gold chain with the big cross
putting on the coat
puffing yourself up
making the sign of the cross:
costume design

strutting out the door and taking up position on a street corner
repeatedly leaving the street corner
going back to the street corner where some of the scorched bags may or may not be
concealed
repeatedly leaving the street corner:
choreography

grinning with the mouth in which some of the other scorched bags may or may not be
concealed
nodding at customers

flashing a gold tooth
nodding at colleagues
nodding at surveillance cameras
looking just angry enough to intimidate but not angry enough to get arrested:
method acting

making a grown man take off his shoes because he's a euro short
sending a desperate woman to a clothing store with a shopping list because
one of your women has a birthday coming up
making a grown man take off his pants for entertainment
getting a grown woman to pay in kind out of boredom:
audience participation

irony:
swallowing the supply when danger looms
understanding what danger is
thinking you're not it

making the sign of the cross
kissing the cross on your chain
thanking the Lord for His protection while heading home

seasoning

pepper
comes from a tropical vine that requires shade, lots of water and high temperatures
pepper
develops as spikes of berries that first turn green, then red and finally black
like us

this salt
comes from the himalayas
it's three million years old
salt always comes from the sea
like us

the extraction yield of a product tells us how easily the taste
of one product transfers to another
we are products
our extraction yield is low

like garden herbs, it is better not to cook us
we are garnish

we are like cloves
cloves are actually flower buds, but that sounds too cute
if you press hard enough, you can stab us into soft flesh

nutmeg used to be exorbitantly expensive
for the price of one nutmeg you used to be able to buy a slave
the purchaser would flaunt his wealth by carrying the nutmeg around with him and
pulling it out in public to flavor his drinks

mace is the aril of the nutmeg
an aril is a seed covering
nobody can flaunt their wealth with a seed covering

only the final frame is black

my double wears a uniform of sweats
first she's a playground
then a harpoon

in this scene my double's waiting for the money
she looks at her phone
her credit has run out

in this scene she meets
the blond boy with the scooter
she follows the loose cannon
through the revolving door

in this scene she has
a soft spot for the dealer
tenderly she strokes
the tattooed tears on his cheek

in this scene my double is hopeful
she has another baby
she buys a pit bull

in this scene my double's a little heavy
she wears a gold name necklace
to five different temp agencies

in this scene she's in a waiting room
she looks humble, meek
an official takes her to task

in this scene my double buys sneakers
she lets her shoulders slump
she hides the mail

in this scene my double gets a ticket
she wears a mask in this scene
i come on

attributes

children   □ yes □ no

sympathy for the sorrow of the involuntarily childless woman   □ yes □ no

sympathy for parental exhaustion   □ yes □ no

cargo bike   □ yes □ no

surplus of abstract knowledge that is difficult to apply to everyday life   □ yes □ no

culinary pretensions mortgage vegetable garden   □ yes □ no

recycling bins   □ yes □ no

ethical consumption   □ yes □ no

comfort shopping   □ yes □ no

festivals overseas travel cerebral secularized meditation weekend mind-expansion

ironic Jesus jesus sandals online activism the country is full everyone's welcome existential crisis

soapbox   □ yes □ no

survival of the fittest   □ yes □ no

exhibitionism   □ yes □ no

marriage   □ yes □ no

polyamory   □ yes □ no

monogamy with extension clause   □ yes □ no

crippling nuance   □ yes □ no

getting yours   □ yes □ no

vernissages belief in your own potential exhibitions success forming cliques around

matters of interest such as conceptual art minimalist interior design indie pop and

the consumption of organic seasonal vegetables prepared according to vegetarian recipes

promoted by trendy cooks yes yes yes   □ yes □ no

photographing meals   □ yes □ no

dates smashed avocados figs cashew cream coffee beans or possibly raw chocolate sourced fairly from south american farmers industrial design cafés yoga wanderlust showing off your impeccable taste obscure bands artists parties more money more stuff more experiences not a job but a calling nostalgic craft berlin for inspiration scandinavia for style saying what you think doing what feels good historical awareness semi-ironic cultural relativism more humanist than feminist free-floating moral indignation self-acceptance self-development belief in your own uniqueness snowflake generation ☐ yes ☐ no

are you sure? ☐ yes ☐ no
daddy was a baby boomer ☐ yes ☐ no
how did mom get on? ☐ yes ☐ no

25 scenes in which the circumstances did not apply

1.

in the light of a lamppost, a black fence in the background, wearing a long, fabulously
well-cut black coat, feet in leather boots, 6'4" over me, he is a pylon

in his eyes all princesses locked behind heavy-lidded eyes he turns to catch
the silent moonlight so i can shudder at how dark they stay
he tells me his name is meat because he eats meat because he's from the mountains
he calls me lola he predicts i will regret everything i don't do
he can't know that i tell him
my name is dolores and i'm not thinking of anybody

2.

the woman's loss has been written in an impossible script
there are rules for dealing
the first rule is tears
must flow and she's only allowed to weep from her eyes
all other methods are wrong

3.

my personal ad has been reduced to the essence:
fem. wants to laugh
lol

4.

on a dark city square on a cold saturday night just before the start of spring
i ask a man with a trumpet to play me the saddest song he has left in his heavy lungs
in exchange for what?
in exchange for nothing
i'm not offering anything i'm not thinking of anybody

5.
i tell an irishman i came for his divine greek ass and stayed for the holes in his pants
he laughs he doesn't believe me he doesn't believe in imagery i say
mutual objectification is a form of equality and i'm not thinking of anybody

6.
i get a face—with glasses—tattooed on my privates
you have to get very close
to see if it's a woman or a man

7.
i stop shaving
i buy a trimmer
my slit is a statement
i keep everything short
because that is genuine

8.
i ask a religious man how long his
beard can grow he suggests we be idle together to find out i have forgotten why
idleness is the devil's playground and i'm not thinking of anybody

9.
a kiss turns out to be a way of eating someone and the train station looks odd
when you're munching away at a stranger on the platform without thinking of anybody

10.
i tell a lady from the far north that i smoke i am harboring a grudge my brain is tired and my
flesh is weak
i send her songs filled with the most beautiful bits of my sadness she finds me she finds me
beautiful she decorates me with glitter and gleam calling me intense intense i shine i beam
she has invented me

11.

a surly hermit asks "shall we start over?"

i tell him he has to read lolita he asks if the film is based on it i say the book is better of course

he thinks i'm beautiful when i put my hair up

he's only read dostoevsky

i don't know what that says about him but i'm not thinking

of anybody

12.

to a creature who claims to be sapiosexual i say less and less

she says she prefers to keep her love free

i tell her dogs like to play with frisbees

she asks if my love is a boomerang too i say

my love

is an asphalt highway the asphalt is still hot but i'm not thinking of anybody

13.

a doll with a perforated lower lip tells me her menstrual cup is too small for her flow

i say my friday's already taken

14.

to the man with the black bar over his eyes

i say that i wish

someone had told me that mathematics can lead to superior abstraction

he says you're better off being alone if you expect a lot from life

15.

i call the boy with the red scarf round his head rambo despite the lack of muscle tone

he says he knows i know that bodies are only husks driven by urges he is writing

his thesis on cashew nuts in southeast asia i've never been there i'm not thinking of anybody

16.

the socially mobile philosopher doesn't feel at home in his gray
country of birth he misses the warmth
of the working-class neighborhood he didn't feel at home in either
he romanticizes the third world i say
i'm off my rocker give me your money the color falls off my body and underneath i'm
blacker

17.

a nymph tells me today is just perfect for the combination winter coat plus scarf plus sunglasses
i tell her the woman next to me at the bus stop is a redhead
and that i recently read an article about the postpartum recovery of the female body
and in that article a gynecologist said that redheads have a more difficult time in that area
because the recovery of vaginas is a question of connective tissue: something redheads are
generally less
well-endowed in
she doesn't answer

18.

a young underachiever in a village
(which isn't a village because there's a movie theater next to the pancake house)
wants to marry me ironically
he asks if he can go bare chested on the wedding card
i tell him i'm going as saint nicholas and he can go as black pete because that is cutely racially
sensitive
he laughs
i'm not laughing with anybody

19.

a frenchman says he wants to spend a night inside me
i ask if he knows the joke about the *negerin* who went to paris

20.

at one o'clock in the afternoon a viking tells me he just woke up
he was asleep on an electric blanket

i ask is an electric blanket a kind of capitulation
is it an expression of loneliness
does he live in a house without heating
or is he still thinking of someone?

21.

a single mom gives me her definition of love her love
is a pleasant silence
i hear the annoying buzz of negative space

22.

the scientist ignores the functioning of my prefrontal cortex
but if necessary he will pay for dinner
i think about what it would feel like to stroke a cloud

23.

a soldier says meow
i hiss

24.

a silhouette reads to me every night from the work of dead polish poets
they are humanists
they are all thinking of others

25.

by the light of a lamp from the sixties
in the semidarkness
where nobody else is present

i seek you in the city

first i seek your body in the city
i don't find it of course but i'm not in a hurry so
i patiently unscrew body parts from passersby and quietly use them
to assemble yours
i manage pretty well
i only need the color

i seek your color in the old brick paving of a dead, crowded street
i seek you in the polished rails the train glides over
i seek you in crow charcoal asphalt and everything black
between 7 and 8 in the morning i find you on the skin of the electric wires over the entire city
i go up on tiptoes but still can't reach

you are in the hair of the woman crying in church, the beards of pious men, the soles of the shoes
of the girl in the grass, the window frames of the old building where a bride is
posing for a photographer i find you
in bark tree trunks rocks and the sand at three different locations in my country of birth but
customs won't let me take your color back

i find you by the sea on the piles under the pier of course
i find you by the sea
first on the wing of a hungry gull
then i find you
above the sea
in the night that falls
to be like you

forgotten contraband

for instance, a small hard stone in the chest that keeps
growing layers and by accretion defeats
the body around it

the growing stone radiates punishment
to the limbs
to the body the body
protects the constantly growing
stone by hardening around it

the stone hisses through the callused flesh
until the deformed body turns to stone

lead

fired long ago paused come to a standstill just in front of her face staying true floating in front of her nose so she could continue to smell the danger in the thick clouds of gray around her gathered round her they are dark when she touches them they are satin her skin a colorless sensory organ with no history she didn't dream she didn't dream of people armies of bodies in her flesh whereupon her skin became skin again gained color and content a homogenous mass of gases all under pressure her ears crackled she heard drums her eardrums tore, but not from the sound of their footsteps their fingers were not inside of her not in her ripped earlobes it wasn't their doing it was the gold earrings she had hung from her ears to look like her grandmother of course her head was heavy from all that gold she wasn't dreaming when she discovered that she herself was bruising beauty softness body body body subject to time time always haunting time that dries all wounds and repeats repeats repeats she knew her body thanks to her determined muscles she also knew all other bodies and she knew: her mother's knife was no longer planted in her father's side because her father's bones were no longer draped with his flesh because time and the death of all things the smell of lead spoke to her least of all she spent the whole day looking back (that gives a woman a neckache) she only asked to be whole (prayed for it) the presence she invoked ignored her she didn't dream she didn't know how to end serious communications how to leave a room without destroying it the difference between a womb and a tomb after conception where to leave the body how to leave the body

> it's not a breathless threat, the doctor said
> it's a form of rsi that is relatively rare in these parts
> another symptom is that the patient no longer dreams

stormproofing

anchor the body
mortar the feet to bricks and put them in touch with what's under
the earth where all is peaceful and breathing, unmoved
—your heaven is deep below your heaven is hot—

breathe in and out until the bricks are firmly grounded
then take the collected metals
reinforce the legs
fix them in the bricks
use force if necessary

pour concrete over it—you have to do something—
use force where possible
aimlessly beat the base with a hard object
start again if it falls over

thank the gods
then resume at the crotch
pack it, close it off
the aim is to cut off all circulation before turning to the gut
this can cause problems but don't worry it too can be smothered

pour ice water into the pharynx just to be sure
wait for the internal temperature to drop
this process may need to be repeated

observe the storm the storm can no longer touch you
lament the victims
woe is them woe is them

demonstrable effort made

the applicant is better—or at least as good as she's going to get—
virtually free of grammatical errors
sounds like a newsreader
keeps—inasmuch as possible—her thoughts under control
keeps—to an acceptable degree—her emotions under control

no longer hurls cast-iron objects at troubled men
has forgotten her mother tongue
dreams in the language of the former owner
undresses brothers is fond of sisters open
to blue eyes

the applicant has internalized the corrective voice
is occasionally present in her own body
occasionally addresses her own body
(don't be scared there's no fire here not like that not now not here)

the applicant can ride a bike without training wheels
knows how to adjust clothing to the meteorological conditions
can go outside without a coat when it is 60 degrees
uses the hips less when dancing

the applicant visits the right establishments
has learned to spend an hour over a single coffee in exchange for free wi-fi
earns enough for a macbook
knows which sticker to stick on the glowing apple
has found an appropriate hairstyle
hides her brandmarks

the applicant

has an apartment

has, with inimitable and admirable adaptability, acquired everything she couldn't find outside

the eclectic yet coherent furnishing of her home reveals mastery, possibly even synthesis:

the tropical warmwater fish have found a place in black-and-white photos on the mantelpiece

the fully grown, intelligently positioned cactus clashes harmoniously with the caribbean-blue
accent wall

the previously suppressed colors are now accents in the form of decorative cushions,
throws and wooden rosaries carelessly draped over the furniture here and there a surprise
in the form of a china madonna

room has been made for metal and cane

the lost sun features in this tableau in three objects in three different shades of yellow which
help to ground the whole, namely: couch, flower pot, and the collected works of franz kafka

         important details: the couch is not wrapped in plastic and
        the applicant owns a remarkably large number of palm trees

the applicant makes occasional donations to charities dedicated to the alleviation of

the harrowing suffering of people in distant countries

doesn't know what the people who have fled should do either

is broadly socialized

is skeptical regarding claims that are not supported by scientific facts

is critical regarding science

regularly displays an empathetic somewhat misplaced philosophical view of

the suffering of marginalized groups

doesn't know what to do either

can stay awake in the daytime even in winter

has moderated her tone

controls the anger

has pointed the finger at herself

is prepared to learn how to ride a bike while holding an umbrella
is also prepared to learn how to put a bike on the top rack*

* the applicant can furthermore deal in an appropriate fashion with
thick-tongued merrymakers
the rattling bikes passing by
the trains jolting over the tracks
the ubiquitous concrete
the woman across the road with the drinking problem's bottles smashing in the recycling
young men on scooters
small-town stares
the cargo bikes of dual-income breeders
the bureaucracy
the suburban homes
recreation
the long wait for spring
the sighing blossom
the reddish-brown of the bike paths—no longer recalls blood—
impatient commuters
bricks
beggars
fellow humans out shopping
crowded sidewalk cafés
the longing for summer
the difference between city, province and football fans
the cubes of gouda
the humor of orange afro wigs
the importance of carnival
the ongoing complaints about the weather
the four seasons
the racing cyclists

we welcome the applicant

the rain
the hail
the wind
the newspapers with a cultural supplement
the escalators the hospitality concepts
the parliament
young men with moustaches
young men in leggings
the fraternities
the theaters
the art galleries
the punctuality of the public transport
the sparsity of nature
the full country
the flat, rectangular landscapes
the well-fed cows
the xenophobia
the freeways
the efficiency
the popular press
the suburbs
the windmills
the freedom of expression
the bible belt
the reliable utilities
the commemoration of the dead
the ailing meritocracy
the bildung
the mistrust of the eastern bloc
old men with mail-order brides
the social security
the hitler jokes
the patronizing

the thin walls

the omnipresence of arnon grunberg

the glass ceiling

the consensus

the glorification of malleability

the norm

the worship of unattainable physical beauty

the polemic

the postmodernism

the somethingism

the populism

the calvinism

the capitalism

the nihilism

the hedonism

the sexism

the nationalism

the existentialism

the atheism

the exoticism

the veganism

the feminism

the activism

the relativism

the objectivism

the pragmatism

the hoarfrost

the ground frost

the black ice

epilogue

roosting tree

on my way to the roosting tree i water
and manure one square mile of reddish-brown earth
it's an altruistic investment i'm making it
possible for someone else to put down roots expand disrupt the ecosystem
then i give my hands a good scrub
—long and painstaking—
i peel the prints from my fingers
—careful   i am careful—

i cut my hair because i am a victim
i dye my hair because i am a thug
i cultivate a moustache to match my forged documents
—i am calm   i am calm—

i fly the boeing through the turbulence in retrospect
to the man who casually and unintentionally begot me
i take a hostage, introduce him on arrival saying
this man reminds me of you i don't want him we need to talk it's tragic
that i am going to wear him
and i will wear him
i will wear him like a bearskin like a cloak
his skin smells of desert heat fenugreek and open wounds

i am taking my mother back to the barren land because i love her
for the love of my mother i give all my kin back to the earth i cast off
my cloak because i love my mother because i love my mother i ward off repetition
from my clamped ovaries

my clamped ovaries are clean
my clamped ovaries are magnificent
my clamped ovaries are made of reactive metals

this is where i roost
i rust
i rest here
it ends here

a note from the translator

TRANSLATION IS WRITING WHAT YOU READ. Not "in your own words" like a high-school student or a well-coached witness, but in the words you give to the foreign-language author to become theirs, their voice in English, at least for the work at hand. The idea isn't to make them sound like they come from Illinois or Islington (unless the narrator, character, or lyrical persona comes from Islington or Illinois), but to fashion an authentic English voice that is anchored to a non-English-speaking place, time, society, culture. This is impossible, of course, but like all sleight of hand, the trick is to make the impossible convincing.

An empathetic leap is required, always, but the distance the translator has to cover varies enormously and is determined by much more than just the triad of age, gender, and skin color. The translator's own experience of class, climate, and religion, for example, can mean the difference between an appreciation of particular images that is largely intellectual and one that is rooted in personal, even visceral memories. When does the distance become too great? And at the other extreme, when does identification become too glib? There's a danger of the translator feeling so at one with the author that they stop questioning and start channeling. For all its seductiveness, method translation can be misleading. An overly confident assumption of the author's persona can cloud understanding and set off a slow slide into cliché.

An advantage or annoyance of translating poetry from Dutch into English, depending on the translator's inclinations and the match or mismatch of personalities, is that Dutch-language poets tend to have very good English and are almost always keen to look closely at the translation and engage in a discussion of choices and options. My own experience of these collaborations has been overwhelmingly positive, both personally and in terms of the contribution to the quality of the translation, but this is partly because I have learned to combine a relative openness to discussion with an early clarification that final responsibility for the English rests with the translator (my policy of never agreeing to anything on the spot—"I need to think about that"—became a running gag during my discussions with Fabias, who is an expert at producing a gently mocking "hmm"), and partly because book-length poetry translations have a long lead-in time and almost always emerge from translations of much smaller sets of poems, so that unhappy poet-translator combinations are generally spotted early and shunted off to the side.

With *Habitus* too I was asked to translate based not just on my track record with other poets, but also on my 2018 collaboration with Fabias in preparing translations for a performance at the Crossing Border Festival in The Hague. I was honored but reticent, fearing that, as evocative and powerful as I found the work, too many elements were too removed from my own experience for me to render them effectively. (See "distance to cover," above.) I'd never been to the Caribbean, let alone Curaçao. And, yes, all three of the triad's elements were unfavorable. It seemed to me that the only way to ensure that the phrasing and word choices didn't drift away from Fabias's vision was to establish beforehand that she was willing and able to get involved in the translation under the conditions described above, and it was only after discussing this with her in person that I agreed to sign on to the project. The pandemic intervened and made communication much more difficult, but in the end we were able to go through the whole book in a series of long, fruitful, and very enjoyable telephone conversations.

Curaçao is a polyglot society with Dutch as the administrative language, a large majority of the population having Papiamentu as their mother tongue, and widespread use of English and Spanish. During one of our first discussions, Fabias explained the cacophony of voices that influenced her own language acquisition, with her Spanish, for instance, shaped not just by the Spanish of nearby countries like Venezuela and the Dominican Republic, but also by the Castilian Spanish of the Dutch education system. With English, the situation was even more complex, with her accent and ear tuned by the American English of TV, music, and the tourism industry, the British English taught at school, the Patois of Jamaican immigrants, and the lilting voices of her relatives from St. Martin. She found it important that the English in the book be familiar to readers from Curaçao—without jarring Britishisms (let alone, in my case, Australianisms)—but at the same time it needed to reflect the Dutch of her poetry. She didn't want her poems adjusted in translation to fit sensitivities or a historical timeline that didn't correspond to the realities she describes. Rather than squeezing her poetry into English, the idea was to cut the cloth of English wide enough to fit her poetry. (The trick of authenticity.) This was particularly relevant when it came to choosing how to translate and sometimes not translate words or phrases that relate to sex and racism, and here I deferred wholeheartedly to her preferences and was grateful that she had them, that she'd thought them through and felt them strongly, and that she was happy to explain them to me.

If poetry is the marriage of literary form and content, then poetry translation is the crisis that tests even the strongest relationship. The difficulty for the translator is knowing where to take liberties, when to stray from meaning to maintain form, and how far to go when adjusting form to fit the patterns of meaning in the new language. Ironically, these choices are often much more straightforward when the constraints of fixed meter and rhyme apply. In that instance the execution is difficult, but the task is clear. When the form is looser it's hard to decide what to do. Free verse might be like playing tennis without a net, but it's also a high-wire act where the absence of the net has quite different consequences. In enjambed poetry with irregular line lengths, the specific ambiguities and emphases of the original breaks are often unsustainable in translation, and the translator has to decide when and where to enrich the translation by taking advantage of the new language's often very different potential points of inflection. Here again Fabias was proactive, choosing many times to introduce new line breaks in English that sometimes reconfigured whole sections of the poems. Our discussions took a curious turn here, as I sometimes felt that it was more important to maintain the patterns of the Dutch. In an inversion of what might be expected, the poet argued for more deviation from the original while the translator worried about what was being lost!

This kind of push and pull was characteristic of the whole discussion. Moving away from the line breaks to the words of the translation, we mostly considered liberties I had taken and places where I had deviated from the Dutch. A poetry translator has two chief responsibilities: to represent the original and to turn the translation into a poem in its own right. As much as I was keen to accommodate Fabias's suggestions and wishes in regard to the first, I was also obliged to test proposed changes against the second and resist them when I felt they were compromising the effectiveness of the resulting English poem—all the while trying to make sure I wasn't just being precious or narrow-minded. This meant that I couldn't just say yes to everything ("I need to think about that."), but also that I couldn't ignore any nagging sense of a tweak not being quite right. Fabias was equally persistent ("Hmm . . .") and so we kept worrying at the same words and phrases, returning to them multiple times, nudging them this way and that. And because we were both most interested in the final result, the process could end with me suddenly backtracking to accept her suggestion after all or her encouraging me to resolve a disagreement by trusting my intuition and taking the leap.

The title *Habitus* required no translation. Hopefully the entire book now seems as if it stepped into English just as effortlessly.

David Colmer
January 2021

Radna Fabias was born on the Caribbean island of Curaçao and moved to the Netherlands to study at the age of seventeen. Her first collection of poetry, *Habitus*, was published in 2018 to universal acclaim and went on to win an unprecedented five Dutch and Belgian poetry prizes. *Habitus* has also been translated into French and Italian, with Spanish and German editions in production.

David Colmer is an Australian translator, mainly of Dutch-language literature. His translations in a range of genres have won many prizes, most recently the James Brockway Prize for his work in poetry translation. Colmer's translation of a selection of Mustafa Stitou's poetry, *Two Half Faces*, was published by Deep Vellum / Phoneme Media in late 2020.

Thank you all
for your support.
We do this for you,
and could not do
it without you.

DEEP
VELLUM

PARTNERS

EMBREY FAMILY
FOUNDATION

ALLRED
CAPITAL MANAGEMENT
of
RAYMOND JAMES®

ADDITIONAL DONORS, CONT'D

Mark Haber

Mary Cline

Maynard Thomson

Michael Reklis

Mike Soto

Mokhtar Ramadan

Nikki & Dennis Gibson

Patrick Kukucka

Patrick Kutcher

Rev. Elizabeth & Neil Moseley

Richard Meyer

Scott & Katy Nimmons

Sherry Perry

Sydneyann Binion

Stephen Harding

Stephen Williamson

Susan Carp

Susan Ernst

Theater Jones

Tim Perttula

Tony Thomson

SUBSCRIBERS

Ned Russin

Michael Binkley

Michael Schneiderman

Aviya Kushner

Kenneth McClain

Eugenie Cha

Stephen Fuller

Joseph Rebella

Brian Matthew Kim

Anthony Brown

Michael Lighty

Erin Kubatzky

Shelby Vincent

Margaret Terwey

Ben Fountain

Caroline West

Ryan Todd

Gina Rios

Caitlin Jans

Ian Robinson

Elena Rush

Courtney Sheedy

Elif Ağanoğlu

Laura Gee

Valerie Boyd

Brian Bell

AVAILABLE NOW FROM DEEP VELLUM

FORTHCOMING FROM DEEP VELLUM

SHANE ANDERSON · *After the Oracle* · USA

MARIO BELLATIN · *Beauty Salon* · translated by David Shook · MEXICO

MIRCEA CĂRTĂRESCU · *Solenoid*
translated by Sean Cotter · ROMANIA

LEYLÂ ERBIL · *A Strange Woman*
translated by Nermin Menemencioğlu & Amy Marie Spangler· TURKEY

RADNA FABIAS · *Habitus* · translated by David Colmer · CURAÇAO/NETHERLANDS

SARA GOUDARZI · *The Almond in the Apricot* · USA

GYULA JENEI · *Always Different* · translated by Diana Senechal · HUNGARY

UZMA ASLAM KHAN • *The Miraculous True History of Nomi Ali* • PAKISTAN

SONG LIN · *The Gleaner Song: Selected Poems* · translated by Dong Li · CHINA

TEDI LÓPEZ MILLS · *The Book of Explanations* · translated by Robin Myers · MEXICO

JUNG YOUNG MOON · *Arriving in a Thick Fog*
translated by Mah Eunji and Jeffrey Karvonen · SOUTH KOREA

FISTON MWANZA MUJILA · *The Villain's Dance*, translated by Roland Glasser · *The River in the Belly: Selected Poems*, translated by Bret Maney · DEMOCRATIC REPUBLIC OF CONGO

LUDMILLA PETRUSHEVSKAYA · *Kidnapped: A Crime Story*, translated by Marian Schwartz · *The New Adventures of Helen: Magical Tales*, translated by Jane Bugaeva · RUSSIA

SERGIO PITOL · *The Love Parade* · translated by G. B. Henson · MEXICO

MANON STEFAN ROS · *The Blue Book of Nebo* · WALES

JIM SCHUTZE · *The Accommodation* · USA

SOPHIA TERAZAWA · *Winter Phoenix: Testimonies in Verse* · POLAND

BOB TRAMMELL · *Jack Ruby & the Origins of the Avant-Garde in Dallas & Other Stories* · USA

BENJAMIN VILLEGAS · *ELPASO: A Punk Story* · translated by Jay Noden · MEXICO